Aug '13

a gift from

Gail - Tmp ②

from mr/mr
& Kmauo

My Lithuania

Selected by
Daniela Mrázková and Vladimír Remeš

Thames and Hudson

My Lithuania
Aleksandras Macijauskas

116 duotone illustrations

Texts by Aleksandras Macijauskas translated from the
Lithuanian by Rimantas Skiauteris.

The photograph on the title page of Aleksandras Macijauskas
in a street in Vilnius in 1985 is by Antanas Sutkus.

The photograph (right) of Aleksandras Macijauskas in
the market in 1975 is by Romualdas Požerskis.

All the originals of the photographs by Aleksandras Macijauskas
are in the collections of the Bibliothèque Nationale, Paris,
and are reproduced by permission of the Conservateur en Chef
of the Département des Estampes et de la Photographie.

The photographs were all taken between 1966 and 1986,
and the texts were written and edited before Lithuania's
declaration of independence on 11 March 1990 and subsequent events.

First published in the United States in 1991 by
Thames and Hudson Inc., 500 Fifth Avenue,
New York, New York 10110

Library of Congress Catalog Card Number 90-70291

Printed and bound in Japan by Dai Nippon

CONTENTS

INTRODUCTION

Dear Daniela

I'm not very used to talking about my private life. All that matters is there in my photographs and in what I've written at the beginning of each section of this book. But if the pictures and commentaries aren't quite enough, here's an attempt at a *curriculum vitae*. It'll be different from what's usually written for such purposes: let's say this is the unofficial version.

I was born in 1938 in Kaunas, then the capital of Lithuania. I don't remember my father at all. He was a professional soldier and even my mother didn't see him often. In 1945, at the very end of the war, he was killed by the Gestapo in Latvia. The circumstances of his death are still obscure.

The end of the war found us struggling to survive in a famine. My brother and I used to spend whole nights queueing in front of closed shops to buy bread in the morning. In summer we lived with my mother's parents in the country, where I herded cows and my brother worked in the fields.

School was a problem. People knew that I had literary aspirations, but although I was good at reciting poetry I was also something of a hooligan. Yet my teachers tolerated me and even went out of their way to be kind because I regularly won competitions for reciting poetry and my own compositions were considered well written.

My mother didn't have much time for me because she was working flat out to earn a living as a washerwoman. It left her dead tired at the end of the day, her hands raw from the soap she used. She often gave me a good thrashing. I deserved it, for I was a bit of a monster, as she said to me one day long afterwards, when we were reminiscing: 'You know, my son, there were times when I begged God to take you.' Yet she sacrificed herself for me and my brother. She had been a beauty once, but now she had no personal life at all.

At fifteen, I used to roam the streets with my mates, but in the evenings, when the day's trouble-making and fighting were over, I wrote verse. In fact I even wrote first thing in the morning and during breaks between lessons. When I had filled a thick notebook I gave it to a lady doctor who had seen me a few times when I'd broken a bone.

7

I think I must have grown up when I did my national service – I passed out first in my flying class. To while away the time I wrote love letters for my mates in the service: the cornier their requests, the more fervour and passion I put into the writing. I had a really imaginative turn of phrase!

After my marriage it came as quite a shock to see life through the eyes of an industrial worker. I got a job in a factory manufacturing lathes and even became quite a good milling-machine operator. I tried my hand at verse again, but the scathing comments I received from editors of magazines crushed me so much that I gave up. As it turned out, I could live without poetry, but I found I couldn't survive without photography. It was photography that made me not merely a responsible citizen but also a real human being.

At the end of 1963 I joined the Kaunas Photographic Club, where there happened to be a great deal of creative talent around. I was totally inexperienced and so I devoted myself to helping with the organization and so on, but at the same time I made a serious study of photography as an art. After six months I brought a portfolio of my work to show at the club. They refused to believe that I'd actually taken the pictures and accused me in front of everybody of buying them somewhere else and passing them off as my own. It was a blow that would have finished many people, but I was used to getting blows. I just obstinately went on bringing in more and more work.

At that time I was living in a single room with my wife, Nijole, and my daughter, Aukse. It had no amenities – no kitchen, nothing – just a tiny room with a smoking coal stove. When I wanted to do some enlarging I had to use the entrance hall. The whole street knew when I was working, because my wife and daughter had to use the window to get in and out.

In 1967 I won a competition and was hired as a reporter by a local evening paper. At first I had a terrible time and kept telling myself that I should stop and go back to my factory job. But my pride prevented me, and I stayed. When I got used to newspaper work I began to enjoy myself – in the end I even started to believe that the job was my natural calling. It was at this period – between 1967 and 1973 – that I did my best work on my 'Village Markets' series. I learnt an enormous amount during my newspaper work and I'd be very pleased to see my children having the same experience.

About this time the recently founded Photography Art Society of the Lithuanian SSR (the only organized centre for creative photography in the entire USSR) held its first Congress, to decide about its own future. My friend Antanas

Sutkus, the founder of the Society, managed to convince me that I should leave my job in order to help him. I became the Society's Executive Secretary and travelled all over Lithuania, establishing small district branches. Life calmed down once the Congress was over. The Society survived and developed. The most pressing question for me was how to survive as myself. It was hard to feel independent when working with Antanas, whose organizational genius devours every collaborator. I suggested that we establish a municipal branch of the Society in Kaunas, where I lived, and he agreed.

I started off in a cellar, which for five years was also my studio. The windows were permanently buried under heaps of coal dumped outside the house, which made the room so dark that blinds were unnecessary. Those were difficult times, but they were also richly rewarding. By 1979 we had established a good gallery and had thirty members. In 1985 I opened a photographic school and another gallery. It's true that all this was achieved at the expense of my own work, so that many ideas remained just ideas. Yet I'm not sorry, because somebody had to do all those things.

Still, in spite of being extremely busy, I found time to photograph and even to study. For five years I attended Kaunas University trying to catch up with everything I had neglected when I was young and stupid, studying what was most useful for my work, management and philosophy. Finally I even won official recognition for my photography and between 1980 and 1985 I received various awards and citations from the Lithuanian government.

I hate talking about my photographs: I'd rather listen to the opinions of others, whether critics or ordinary people. But I've always had a clear idea in my mind of what I wanted to achieve. Every project develops at its own pace. It may differ in character from the others, but the form, the intellectual effort and the prerequisites necessary for coping with it are the same in every case. I believe that one day photography will be mankind's most effective means of expression – or art-form, if you prefer. But this will come about only when photography has mastered what is at the moment the preserve of great literature alone: the ability to depict every aspect and every nuance of human character.

Of the multitude of possible approaches to photography, only one is acceptable to me – the explanation of a human being or a human predicament in its entirety, spanning the full range of feeling from the most sensitive shifts of the spirit to the complete hell of the damned, and summing up simultaneously every element of drama, comedy, absurdity, humour and imagination in the

9

subject. I feel that I have come closest to this objective in my 'Village Markets' cycle, whereas I still have some way to go with the 'Veterinary Clinic' series, although it's fair to say that reviewers of my exhibitions in various countries seem to think otherwise.

Am I happy today? I think I am; especially in recent times, when things have been happening in the world. All I ask of Fate is that my health should not fail me. Now I need ten years to devote solely to photography. If I can have them, I shall be more than happy.

That's about it as regards myself, dear Daniela, but I'd like to finish off with a few words about the important influence you and Czech photography have had on my life. From the early 1960s onwards, your magazine *Revue fotografie* was a bible for us Lithuanian photographers and the only school that we had. It opened the doors and windows for us. Like several other photographers, I was recognized first in Czechoslovakia and only subsequently at home. The publication of my first pictures, my first successes and my first prizes all happened there. The government here gave me a decent apartment only when I won a Grand Prix – the Golden Rose – in an international photographic competition held in Ružomberok, Slovakia.

I still cherish your letters in which, in your capacity as an editor, you commented on my first, in many ways naïve, work. Those were the days: I was young and believed that miracles could happen. In fact, a miracle has happened, for my work has found its way into various galleries abroad, into prestigious photographic collections, and has even been exhibited at the United Nations. Only a short time ago I would never have dared even dream of such things.

And my Photography School in Kaunas? It's alive and well and has a flourishing programme. Years ago I dreamt of having a school like this and then spent a long time fighting for its existence. And if one day it turns out that my own photography was just so much humbug, the beautiful house with its school desks, filled constantly by enthusiastic young photographers-to-be, will be more than ample compensation for the work I've done. What, after all, is creative work? I sincerely believe that it is primarily the sovereign presence of mind and heart.

Yours,
Aleksandras Macijauskas
Kaunas, Lithuania

The Plates

VILLAGE MARKETS

In 1968 a former classmate of mine, who was at that time the chief engineer of a large enterprise, invited me to accompany him on a tour of Lithuania's villages in search of interesting people. We travelled in the organization's trucks and dilapidated jeeps, which frequently broke down on remote cross-country tracks and, on more than one occasion, burst into flames.

The villagers received us in a variety of ways: some with curiosity, some barely concealing their irritation, while others would bring presents of eggs or other produce out of apparent sympathy for the pale and gaunt photographer.

One cool Sunday morning we went to the market in Utena to buy something we needed, and this visit proved to be a turning-point in my life. Suddenly I saw that all the people I had been combing Lithuania for were there, all in one place, with their children, possessions and animals, their vices, their kind hearts and their faces. What faces! Impossible to describe them in speech or writing. Here in the market square was everything – work and pleasure, the ritual of buying and selling, the seller's witty patter that the buyer would never forget when putting his purchase to use.

Neither on that occasion nor on many other market days during our tour did the subject of Lithuanian village markets occur to me as a future photographic theme. Only a year later, when my storage space was almost overflowing with market pictures, did I realize that that was where I belonged – among the teeming, animated throng. That was when I set out on a planned artistic progress.

I acquired a vehicle and a driver's licence. I had my share of accidents, but fate preserved me from broken bones.

'At least somebody will find a use for my efforts', I would tell myself mockingly.

Country markets have often been the subject of holidaymakers and week-end photographers. But why was I drawn to them? No publisher or agency had commissioned me for the task, so why indeed? Now, more than twenty years later, I must attempt to answer the question.

The fact is that, every time I came to a marketplace and began to study the future heroes of my photographs, I became firmly convinced that I had met these people before. Take, for instance, this lean old man, straight as a ramrod, with his grey jacket, white shirt and bristling moustache the colour of wheat. Coming up to me, he gently stroked my scanty whiskers and said:

'You should grow such a moustache in some other place, sonny!'

Then he jerked his head up, took a deep breath and roared with laughter. I recognized him. Surely, he was the incarnation of my late grandfather. On returning home, I shaved off my moustache. I always obeyed my grandfather.

13

Behind a row of carts I catch sight of a pair of long, powerful arms lifting a calf, lowering it to the ground, feeling its muscles. Familiar arms, stained brownish-black with earth and tobacco, their veins standing out like furrows in newly ploughed clay. The calf skips about, tugging at the rope by which this huge man, built like a mountain, is holding it. The lively little animal tries to look him straight in the face, but each time the man turns away. I see in him my Uncle Bolius, the village giant, father of five children. This uncle had always been very kind to me, but for some reason I retain a persistent image of him slaughtering a calf. Tears streamed from the silent animal's eyes. Perhaps it was because of the tension, but my uncle's long nose was suspiciously wet – he was crying too. The third person weeping was myself, a child of eight not long after the end of the war. Perhaps this is why the calves in my recent photographs appear so sad, bearing the white stars of destiny on their foreheads.

Near the corner of the square a small, plumpish woman examines my cameras, my muddy, worn-out shoes, my trousers filthy from clambering on and off carts and trucks, from pushing around among cows and calves, pigs and potatoes and God knows what else, a look of sympathetic mockery on her face. It seems she is sorry for me. I expect her to come up to me, thrust a packet of bread and meat into my hands and say:

'Take it home, but share it out fairly with your brother. And don't forget your mother, either! Don't eat it all up on the way!' Of course – she is the image of my grandmother, as kind-hearted as she is fat.

Like thousands of city children growing up after the war, I often felt hunger. Everyone sought his own way to satisfy it. Sometimes I earned a hunk of bread or piece of mutton by reciting poems to the neighbours, who would lift me up on to the table for the performance. I knew a lot of rather coarse poems by heart.

In the summer, my mother used to send my brother and me to our grandparents in the country, where my brother did all kinds of farm labouring while I grazed the cattle. So from sunrise to sunset I was the proud herdsman of grandfather's six cows and his beautiful one-horned bull.

Grandfather was famous throughout the area for his pedigree livestock, and the spacious farmyard, surrounded by its outbuildings, was frequently the scene of animal love-making. On these occasions grandmother would pull the curtains tightly to and forbid the children to go near them. But doors had cracks and youngsters are naturally resourceful, with the result that we would watch with fascination the matrimonial rites of cattle, horses, sheep and even pigs. Grandfather was matchmaker and counsellor as well as bookkeeper. Sometimes eager potential brides would race across the hills and valleys to meet our famous bull on their own initiative. I would then have to act as matchmaker and, afterwards, hold on to the bride until her master arrived to pay for the service. Grandfather would later give

me a share of the money, with the terse comment, 'For your education.'

The beginning of the school year freed me from my cattle-herding duties and from the lengthy daily prayers which grandmother made us say aloud, since the souls of children had to go to sleep without the tiniest trace of sin. When God and grandmother finally allowed us to settle for the night beneath the shelter, among the piles of hay that swarmed with harmless little beetles, grandfather used to inspect the barn, the stable and all the other farm buildings, make the sign of the cross over everybody and everything, then pause and let out a series of loud farts. In the morning, when grandfather roused me from sleep to drive the herd off to graze, I would scrutinize him closely, curious to know where all those farts were stored.

And then there was the stallion, who had sired foals in a dozen neighbouring villages. I never met such a magnificent specimen in any market. I suspect that grandfather loved him much more than he did grandmother, never mind his seven grandchildren. He would even drive to church in his cart alone – the rest of us were all too insignificant in comparison with his splendid steed. However, he sometimes lifted me up on to the rich chestnut back of the horse and let me ride down to the River Neman and back. Those were great moments in the life of my childhood.

There were also two huge hairy dogs the same colour as the stallion. We used to hide in their kennels to escape grandfather's terrible rage, which would erupt whenever he caught us dismantling the arms and explosives that we frequently found in the local valleys, bushes and ditches in the years following the war. Sometimes when herding the cows, we came across not only weapons but dead soldiers, their faces crawling with flies. Then we would scream and run for protection to our all-powerful grandfather. Usually he would simply shake his head, get wordlessly into his cart and go to inform the district Soviet. Back he would come with soldiers, who collected the weapons and blew up the ammunition, causing our house to shake like a sheaf of corn being threshed. Meanwhile, grandmother said prayers for the dead and sobbed silently. I imagined that the house was filled with soldiers with fly-blown faces. I was afraid to close my eyes.

After the summer apple harvest was over, grandmother would send me to Kaunas, to my mother. Puffing up the hills, she would see me to the railway station, helping me to carry the goods that I had earned myself and the money earned by the bull. All of a sudden, she would produce from under her jacket that greatest delicacy of country cooking, a round smoked-meat *skilandis* – a token of her kindness and affection.

Eventually the fighting in the Lithuanian countryside came to an end. Collective farms were set up. After saying goodbye to his stallion, grandfather became bent and haggard; only his eyes and his moustache radiated an angry light. Once when accompanying me to the station, grandmother said,

'What a pity that the Communists came so late. . . . I might have lived like a human being.'

We began to live like human beings in the city, too. Queues at bread shops vanished. A modern Kaunas–Vilnius highway was built through the village, right across grandfather's Yard of Animal Love. Nevertheless, it was in that very yard of my childhood summers, spied clandestinely through cracks in the doors, that another photographic theme, that of 'The Veterinary Clinic', was to be born thirty years later.

31

46

54

SUMMER

We wait all year for the summer holidays to come round, and then suddenly they are upon us. Our whole state of mind is affected as we try to decide on some different way of spending the time, learning something new, seeing something whose existence we had never even previously suspected. It is a time of obsession.

So, to hell with the office work and its endless hustle and bustle! Damn the exhibitions and striving for success! Down with colleagues and also with myself for having let my hair turn grey in the course of duty! Enough! This time the cameras will stay at home. For twenty years they have clung to me like original sin during week-ends and public holidays, while saner citizens have left the tools of their trade behind.

For those who believe in reincarnation, it is plain that photographers must have had a previous existence as wolves. Driven by instinct, they ran in search of prey. Both as hunter and as hunted they ran. The objective always seemed to be almost within reach. Don't stop! Don't stop!

'Don't stop!' I muttered to myself as I drove towards the seaside with my wife and children sitting in silent concentration. In the boot lay a variety of cameras. At the last moment, force of habit had taken control.

One must always commune with the sea alone, in the same way as with a painting by a genius, no matter what the season or the time of day. Only then will it tell you something – perhaps not always something pleasant, but always the truth.

That year the sea and the beach at Šventoji held a lingering smell of oil as the result of a tanker accident in the port of Klaipeda. All the same, the beach was, as ever, like a painter's canvas already rich in colour and detail, although not finally composed.

The beach at Palanga resembles a busy city thoroughfare with its ceaseless competition for space and struggle for a place to rest. There I am continually haunted by the thought that the whole town is inundated with the trashy output of street photographers with their vulgar and ludicrous props. In the summer of 1984 business was booming and mountains of such trivia were being distributed the length and breadth of the Soviet Union. If a connoisseur of art and culture is offended by it, he has only himself to blame. The majority says thank you and pays for the photos, and it is the majority that matters.

A mermaid, created during the tedious winter months by a resourceful individual from Žemaitija, enticed customers to be photographed. The lure was not so much the piece of amber she held in her hand as her naked body, well-shaped breasts, face of a Madonna, dishevelled hair of a whore, sensuous thighs and seductively curved tail. However, it was no easy matter to have one's image perpetuated in the company of this voluptuous beauty.

65

Queues formed all day long from dawn to dusk, while the enterprising but overworked photographer did not even break off for lunch. Today countless family albums throughout the land contain pictures of the comely temptress of Palanga.

I hate divorce. That is why I spent all five days of my seaside holiday in the company of the mermaid.

Day One: Bright and Sunny

Suddenly I heard a yell: 'Toora-loora-loora-looraloo!'

The cry rose from different parts of the beach. Involuntarily my feet carried me towards the mermaid. A group of eleven people was being photographed with looks of concentration or animation on their faces. If anybody closed his eyes with the pleasure of it all, the husky voice of the photographer rang out: 'Toora-loora-loora-loora-loo!' which was his way of saying, 'Don't shut your eyes! Watch the birdie!'

Meanwhile, waiting groups were fumbling with their hairdos and practising earnest poses. A serious ritual was in progress. The photographer from Žemaitija was selling immortality to ordinary working people, and at a very reasonable price. Their great-great-grandchildren would one day gaze perplexedly at these forebears of theirs beside the Palanga mermaid.

However, I felt my chest tightening through a sense of professional vanity and nausea. The surging music of the Baltic surf took on the sound of sickly sentimental crooning. I picked up my cameras and was slowly dragging myself from the beach when a man wearing a black jacket appeared and came in my direction. He was in a hurry, his face taut with anxiety. I realized that he had forgotten something vitally important and could concentrate on nothing but returning to the water's edge. This, at least, was the message he conveyed to the thousand-strong crowd of semi-naked pleasure-seekers on the beach. He ignored the shapely mermaid. All he could see was a rainbow in the form of an enormous question-mark. He strode purposefully towards it. I stepped aside. Maybe I shall see him again tomorrow?

Day Two: A Tiny Cloud

In the morning I got up feeling rather rotten. The scenes that I had witnessed yesterday still lingered in my mind. What was it that attracted all these decent folk to the mermaid? This thought kept humming in my brain like an importunate gnat, and urged my own flabby body to the beach.

This time the sea looked weary and apathetic. Tiny breakers were silently lapping against the mermaid's metal supports. A businesslike lady was forming her family up to be photographed, the last in line being her elderly and indifferent husband.

'Toora-loora-loora-loora-loo!' For a moment the face of the *pater familias* lit up, but only for a moment.

'Jesus! I can't get a decent night's sleep with all this yelling', complained a woman beside me. 'It follows me all over Palanga. What have I done to deserve such punishment?'

'But the photographer's clients are not from another planet', I said with some irritation. 'We reap the fruits of our own upbringing.'

The majority, though, were of a different opinion. You can't get away from noise; it is here, there and everywhere in one form or another. Twentieth-century man is as uncomfortable without noise as he is without his trousers, although what really only matters here is the effect of the sun in tanning the pallid body of the city-dweller.

I looked at my cameras without any sense of pleasure. How long shall I wait for the man in the black jacket?

He turned up towards evening, approaching with the same step, but staring down at his feet. I set the exposure meter, but something prevented me from pressing the button. He must be near to achieving his purpose, I thought; there is no need to invade his privacy. . . I have nothing to do with him, and he has nothing to do with me.

A strange weakness crept into my legs. When I finally steadied myself, the figure of the man in the black jacket was already far away.

Day Three: A Manager and a Breeze
Young and old, sick and healthy, they were all lining up by the mermaid. I tried to guess their jobs, hobbies and nationalities. The photographer might have failed to seduce a few conceited individuals who make a point of behaving differently from others, but there was hardly a representative of any profession who would not have deigned to pose with 'Miss Palanga 1984'.

A stranger settled down beside my equipment. He studied the people roasting in the sun with an eagle's eye, cast a critical glance at my cameras and frowned in deep concentration.

'A born manager', I concluded.

He was clearly a newcomer to the beach, determined to find peace and quiet. Naughty children were immediately reprimanded; space was established between the inert sunbathers and the active groups; even the irritating music sounded fainter. The beach was becoming orderly. After a while, he stretched out, satisfied, on the sand, his completely bald head glistening in the sun. His fierce eyes, accustomed to dominating subordinates and even strangers, turned to scrutinizing the mermaid. Dough-like strips that had once formed muscles hung from her arms and were set in motion by the breeze, creating a mournful sound.

'Toora-loora-loora-loora-loo!' sang out the photographer.

With a glance, the manager gathered up his wife and a troupe of children from the sand, indicating the mermaid. In an instant, the whole family was posing in a disciplined group.

'I'd like to see him arrange his own funeral', I thought unkindly.

In the distance I caught sight of the man in the black jacket. Today his head was raised and his

stride was steady. I lifted my camera and took the shot.

Twins from Kaunas were drowned that day.

Day Four: Eating and Drinking

We have a popular game, 'hospitality *à la Lithuanienne*'. Its rules are stunningly simple. At a table laden with food and beverages, you have to pretend to be worried by the lack of anything to eat or drink. The more delicately this is done, the more successful is the entertainment.

The game does not go down so well on the beach, although it is the scene of constant eating. The fact is that the shedding of clothes reveals evidence of a fondness for food so shamelessly that the tongue simply cannot find the right words to express the idea of any shortage.

As though to set them an example, a former competitive athlete runs past the gluttons. My camera has already followed him for several days, but he races by too fast to enable me to take a photograph. Through the blur of his body, the sky and the beach can be clearly seen. I wished I could also see the heart that had been propelling him over the surface of the earth for all those years.

'Toora-loora-loora-loora-loo!' cried the photographer, and the man increased his speed. The mermaid was hardly visible today among the crowd. Only occasionally could one catch a glimpse of her sickly sweet face and her breasts being stroked by two grinning drunkards from the south.

Suddenly the man in the black jacket stopped in front of me. It was the first time that I had seen him so close, and I was conscious that his face radiated wisdom and power. Holding his hand beneath the lapel of his jacket, he inspected me for a moment and smiled proudly. As he walked away, I couldn't tear my eyes away from the man's feet. Rhythmically they seemed to measure the passing of the summer – his own and perhaps mine also. Time was passing inexorably. Only one more day to go.

Day Five: Clear and Cloudless

The sun had turned my body into a badly grilled steak that moved awkwardly on lily-white legs. Did I belong here, the inquisitive fellow with the camera? Such people should be put in their proper place, the born manager would surely have said.

I felt certain that the man in the black jacket would not return. Yesterday I realized that there had been a change in him. Perhaps he had found, or had remembered, the missing thing? But then, why did he say nothing? Had the bossy manager banned him from the beach? Or had he simply taken off his jacket and faded into the crowd?

Goodbye, then, 'Miss Palanga'! Goodbye, resourceful photographer from Žemaitija! My heartfelt thanks for your wonderful theatre of the absurd. During these five brief days of summer, thousands of players have acted out their parts beside the mermaid. It is said that there are still some individuals to be met. But perhaps I have misunderstood something here. Perhaps.

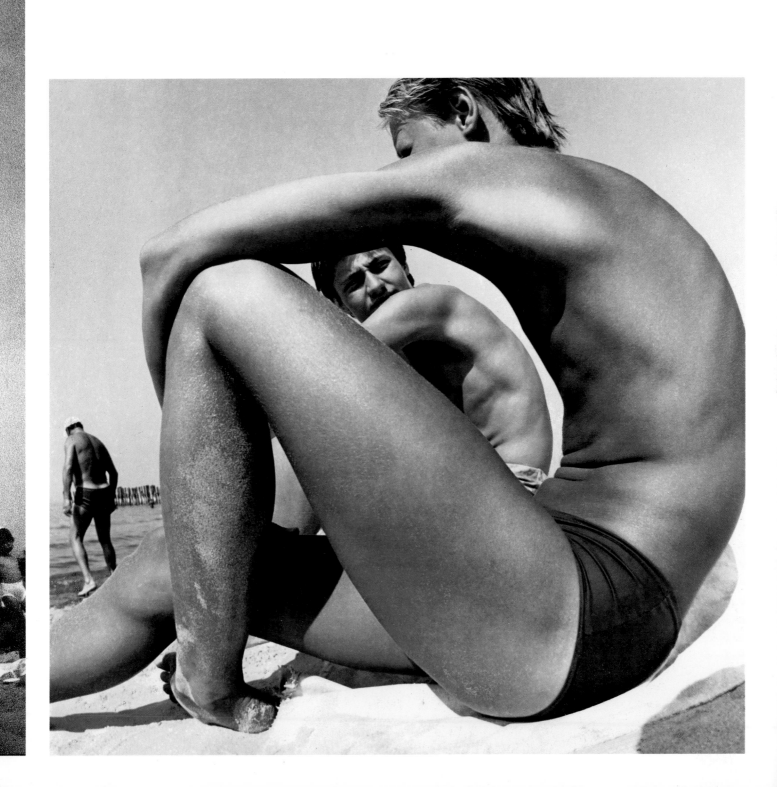

THE
VETERINARY CLINIC

In 1977 I was invited, as an artist, to a meeting at the Kaunas Veterinary Academy. We were talking about my 'Village Markets' series when one of the students remarked.

'Even the stench of manure seems real in your market photos.'

'And of a dog's kennel', I agreed.

'Why don't you try our clinic?' suggested one of the teachers. 'It's your kind of theme.'

He was right. The subject suited me perfectly.

What does veterinary work mean to me? Rescuing countless animals, both wild and domestic? Saving vast sums of state investment in livestock? Scientific research and discovery?

None of these things. They are all the business of economists, scientists and sociologists. They mean virtually nothing to me. My interest lies in the spirit that guides the healing hands of the aging, angular veterinary surgeon, the spirit that lights on the inquiring faces of the students and fills the pleading, pain-racked eyes of the suffering white cow with hope.

At the height of a wintry February storm, with the roads buried beneath the snow, this cow was brought to the clinic on a horse-drawn sleigh by the chairman of the collective farm himself. For several days she had been trying to calve. The operation was successful, the calf was safely delivered, and the face of the exhausted chairman glowed with joy.

Sometimes I would accompany the surgeons to watch operations on horses and other animals on the farms. The stallion that was to be gelded was very big, and consequently very confident. He must have loved and trusted people, because he made no resistance to being tied up and operated on. But when he was set free, all the fields and countryside around reverberated with his neighing. No, not neighing; rather, lamentation, reproach, grieving for the loss of passion, strife and love.

We avoided each other's eyes. Without a word, we got into the car and left.

'He has cursed us', said one of the surgeons.

And so it is that veterinary work means more to me than simply figures, registers and economics.

85

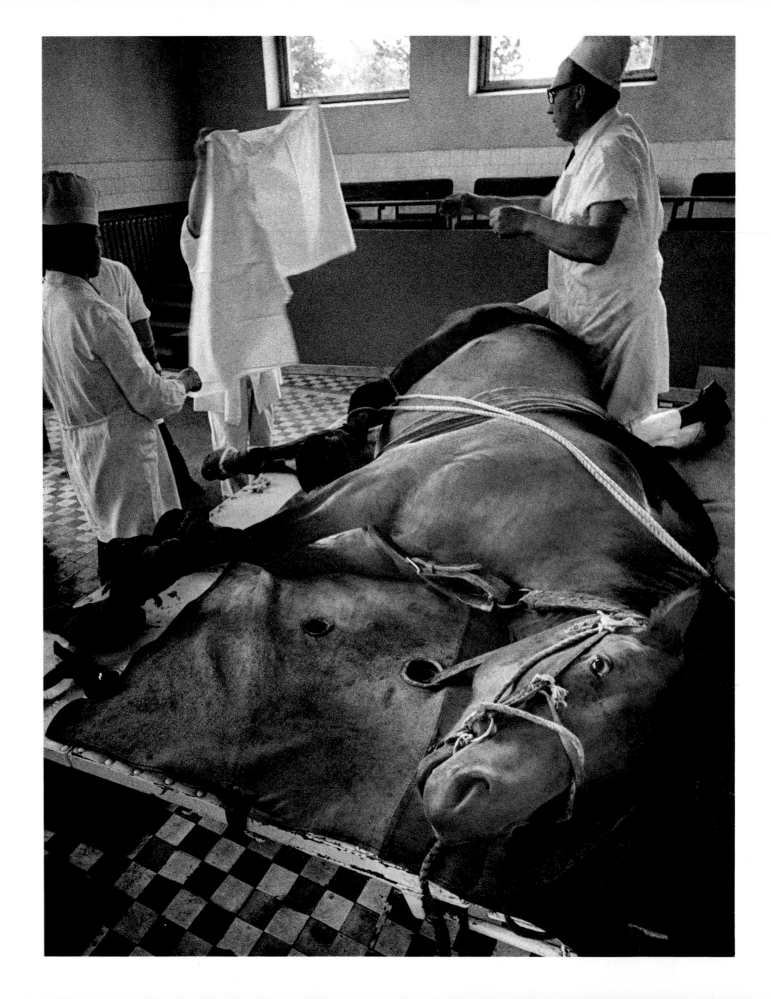

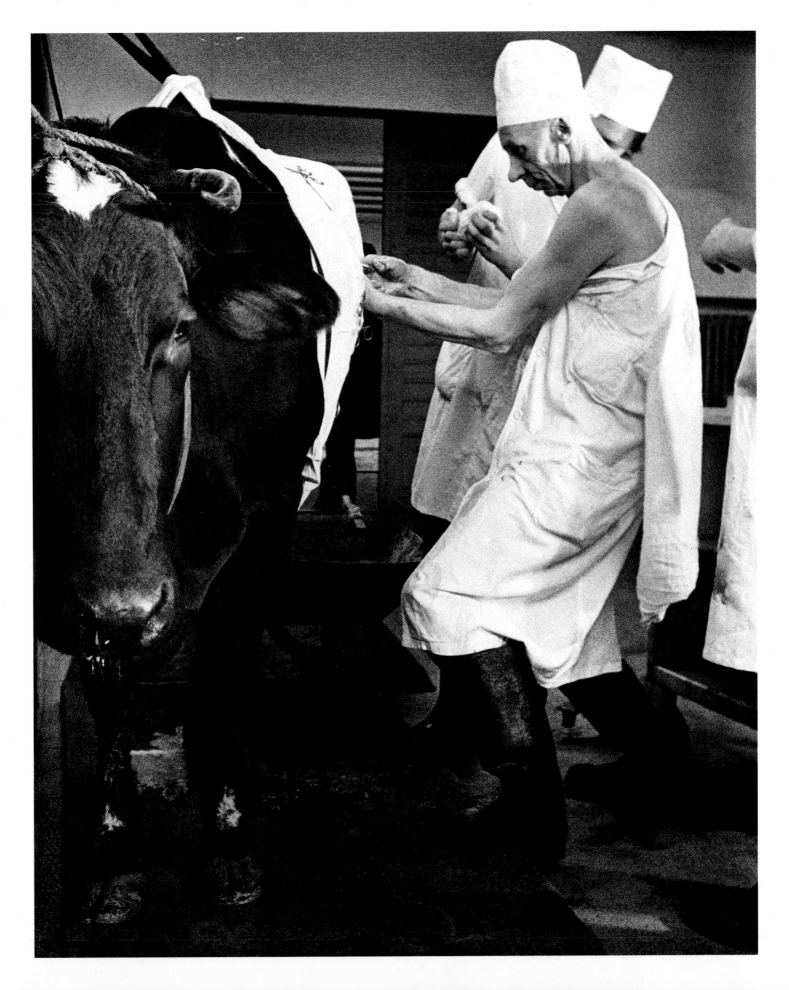

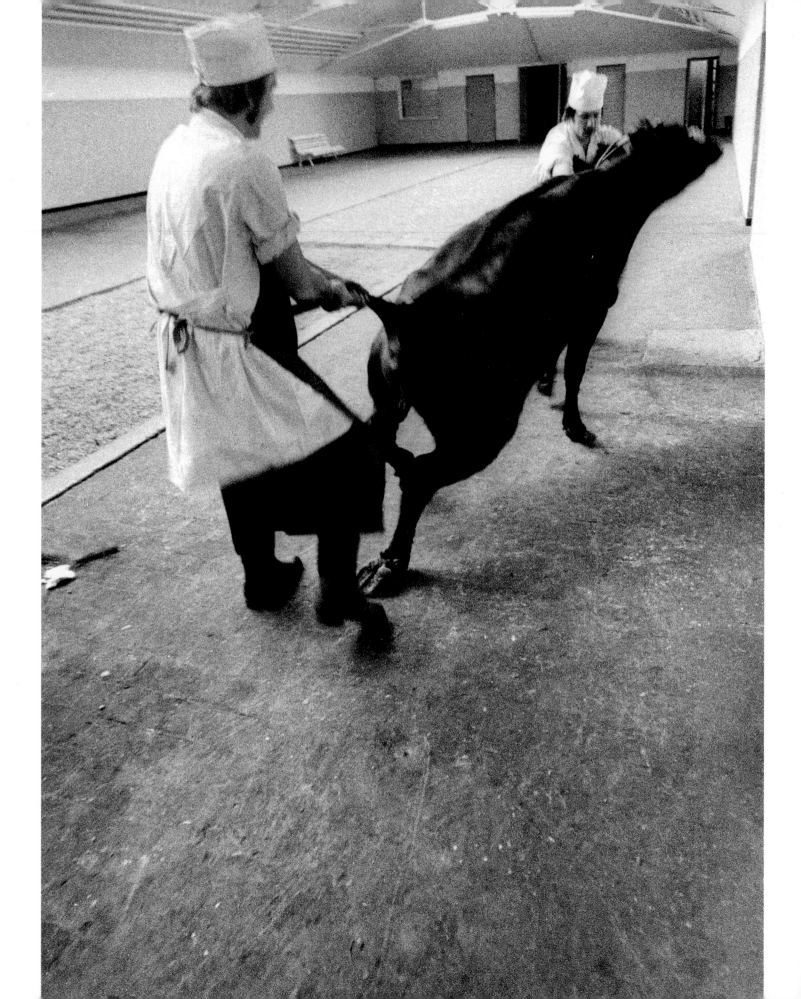

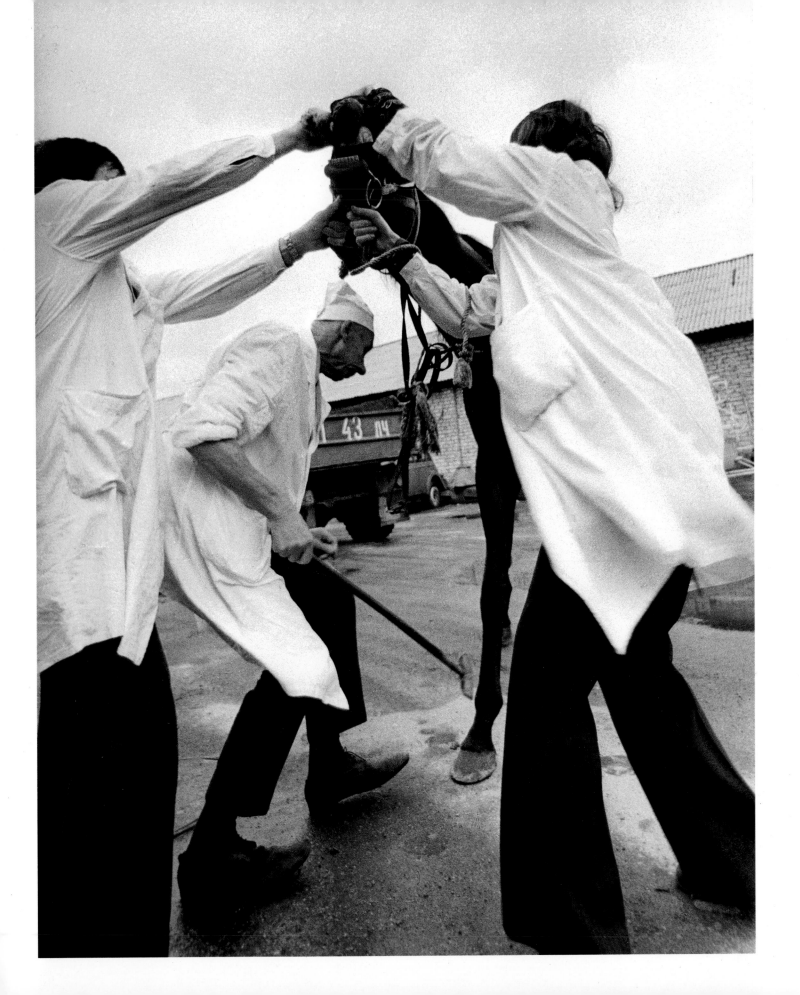

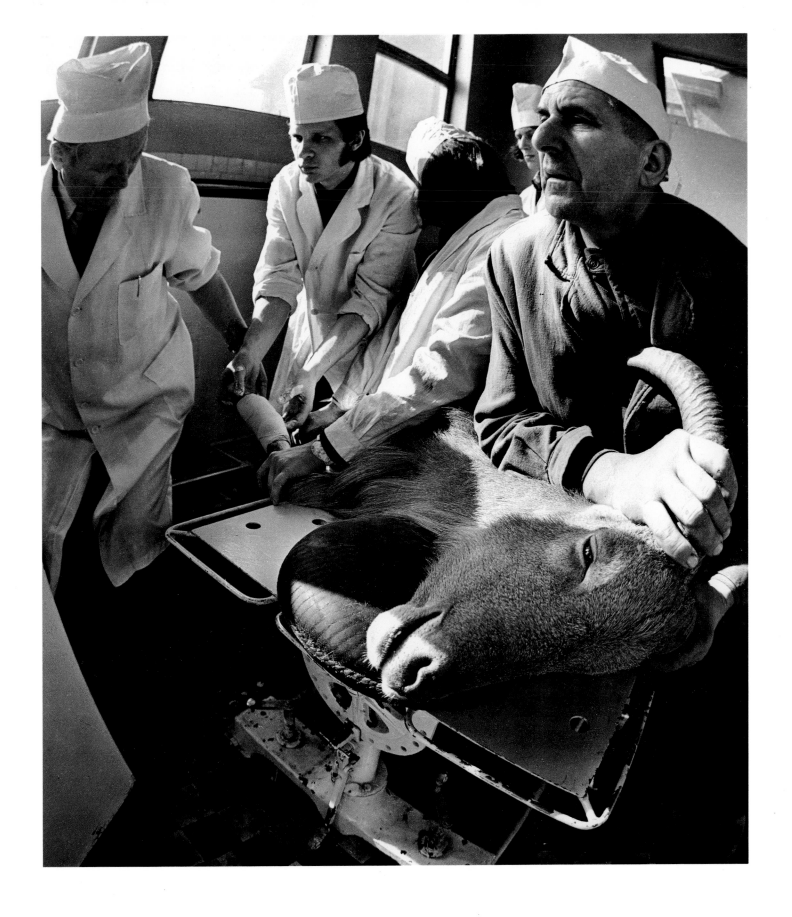

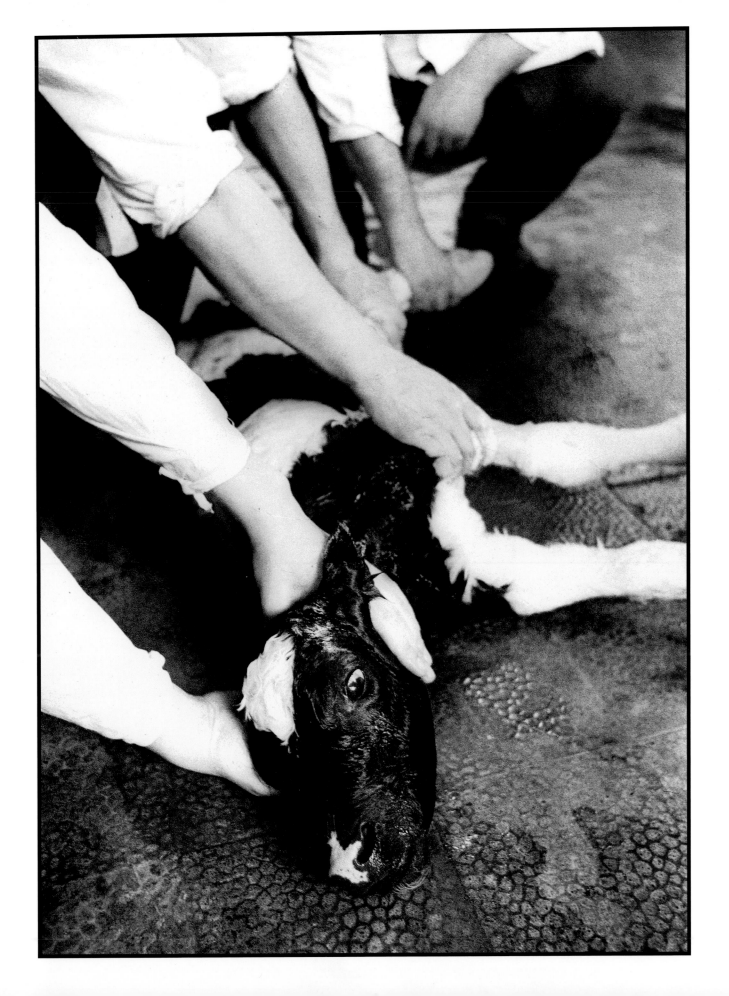

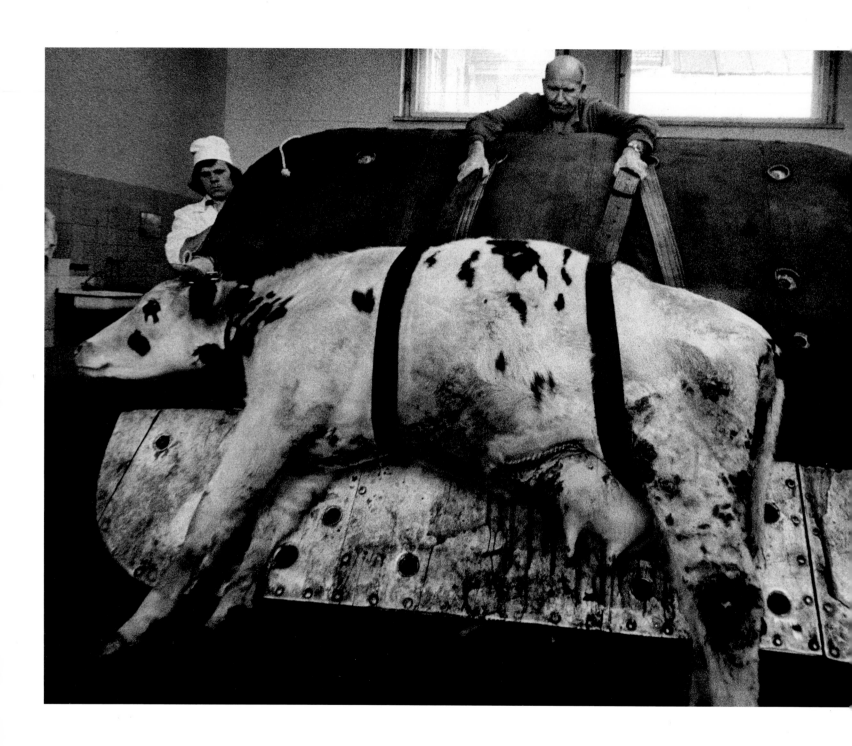

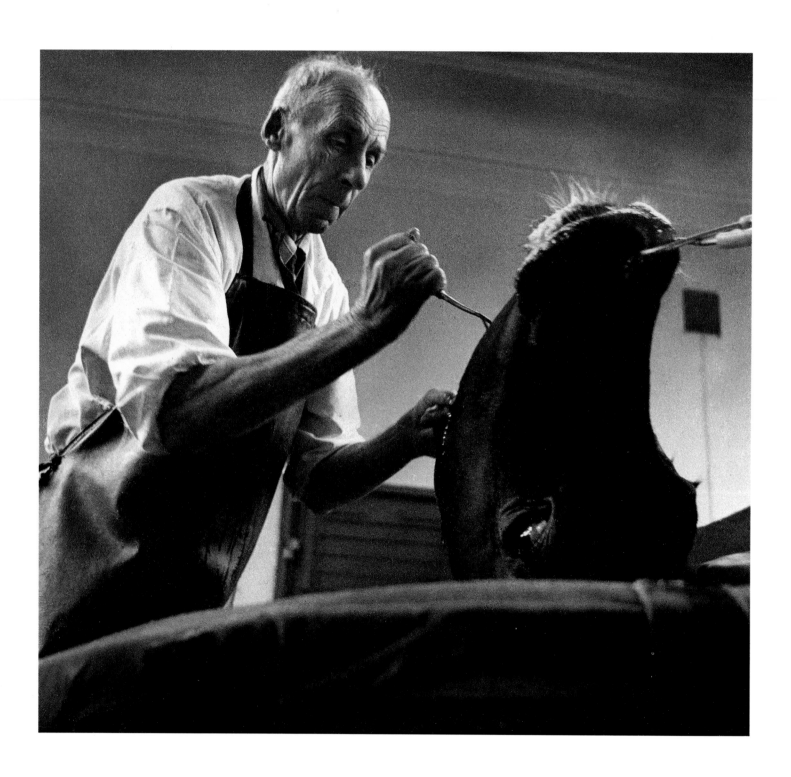

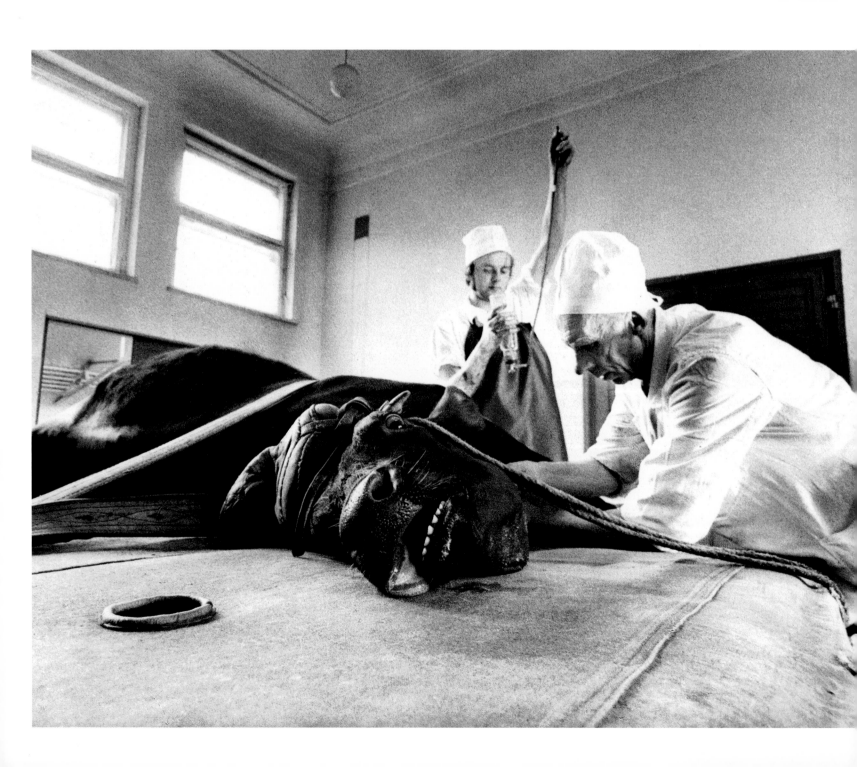

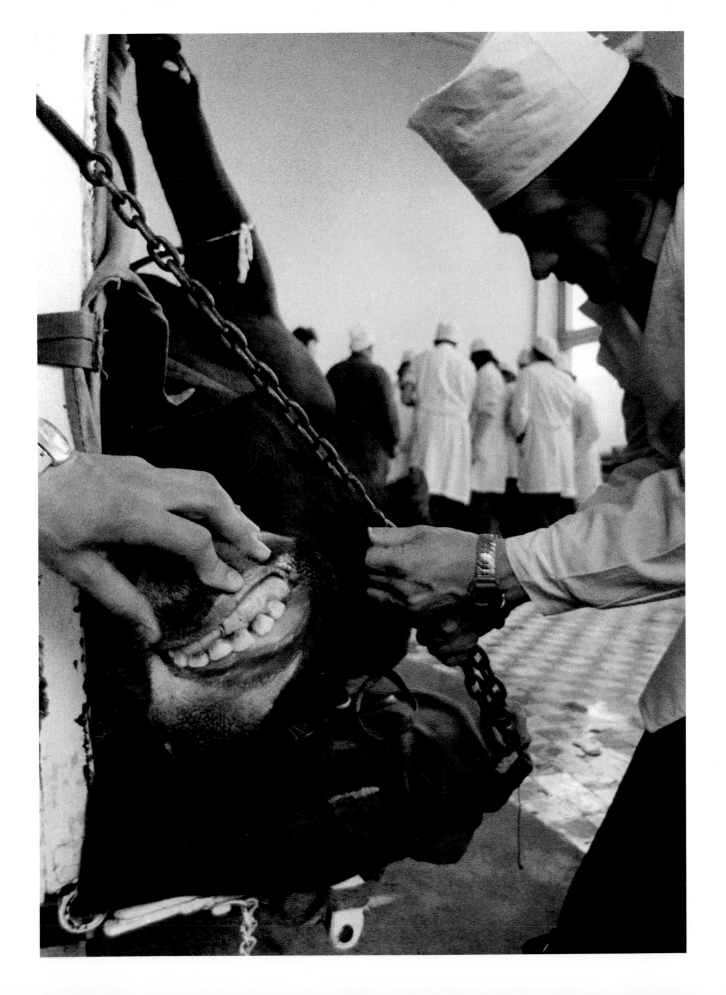

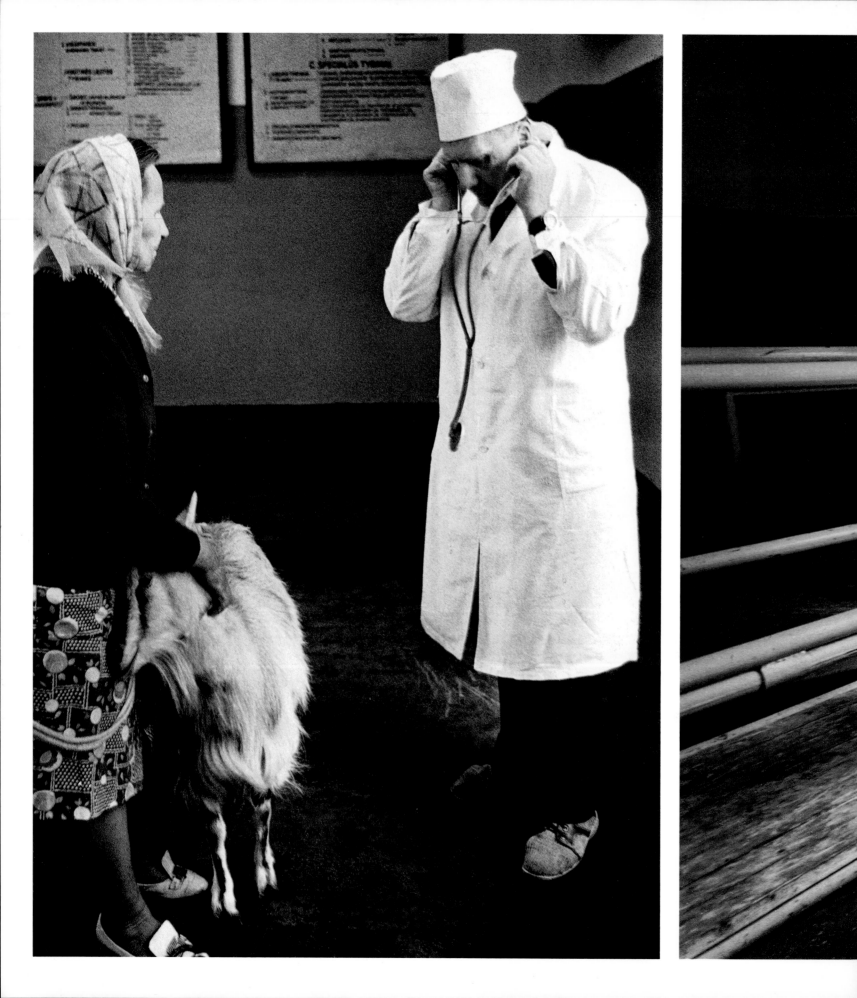

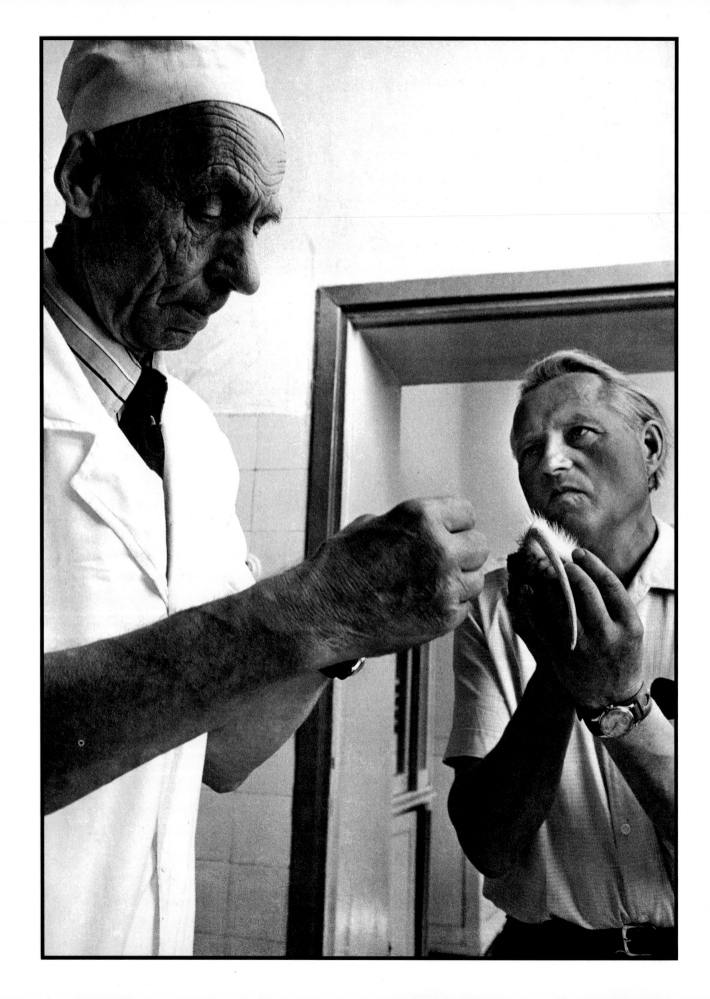

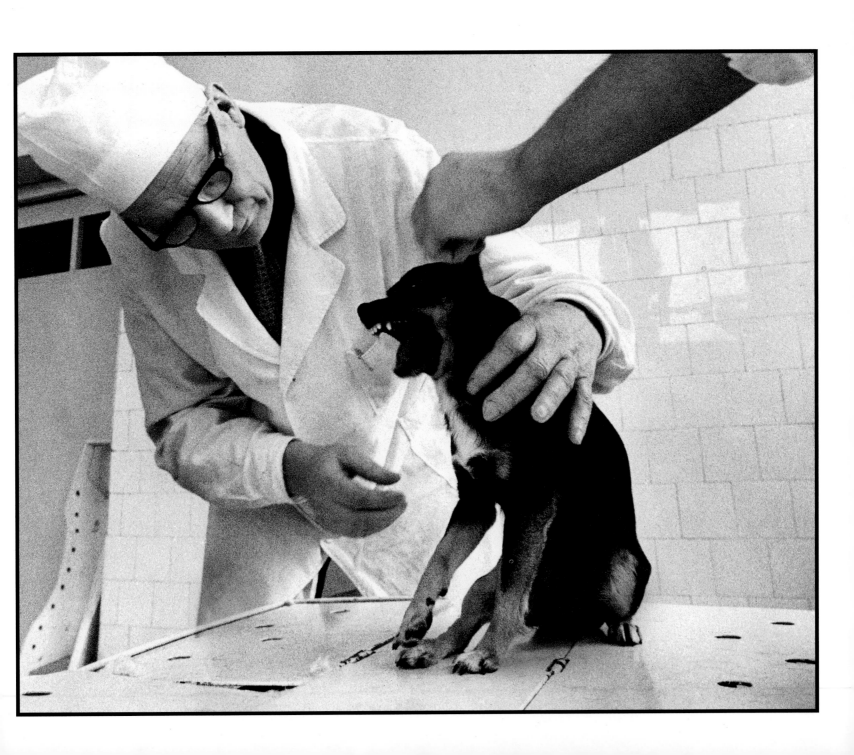

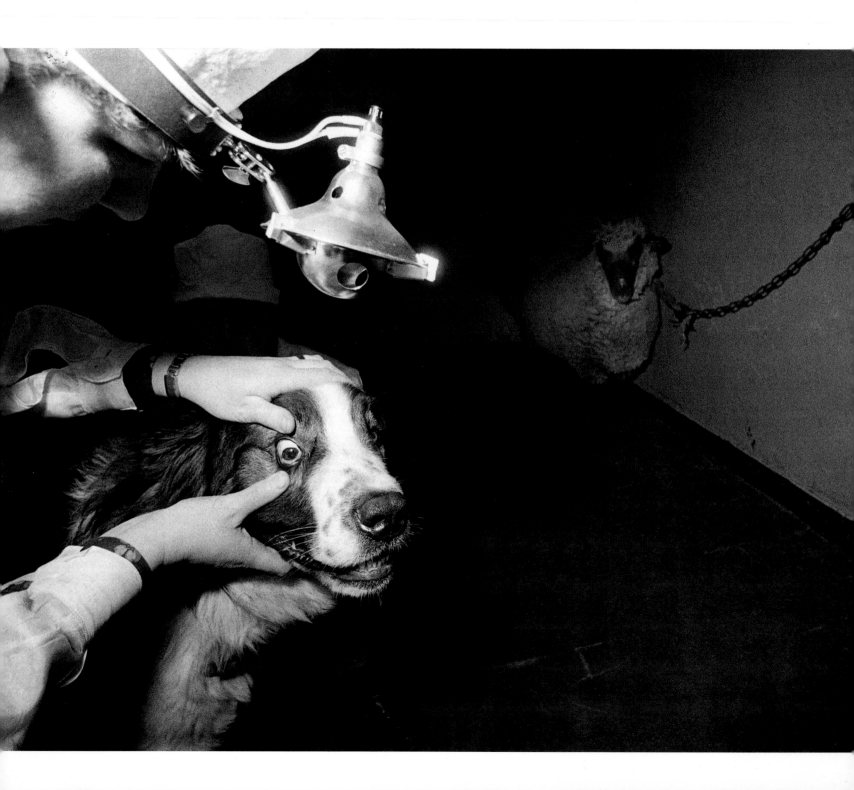

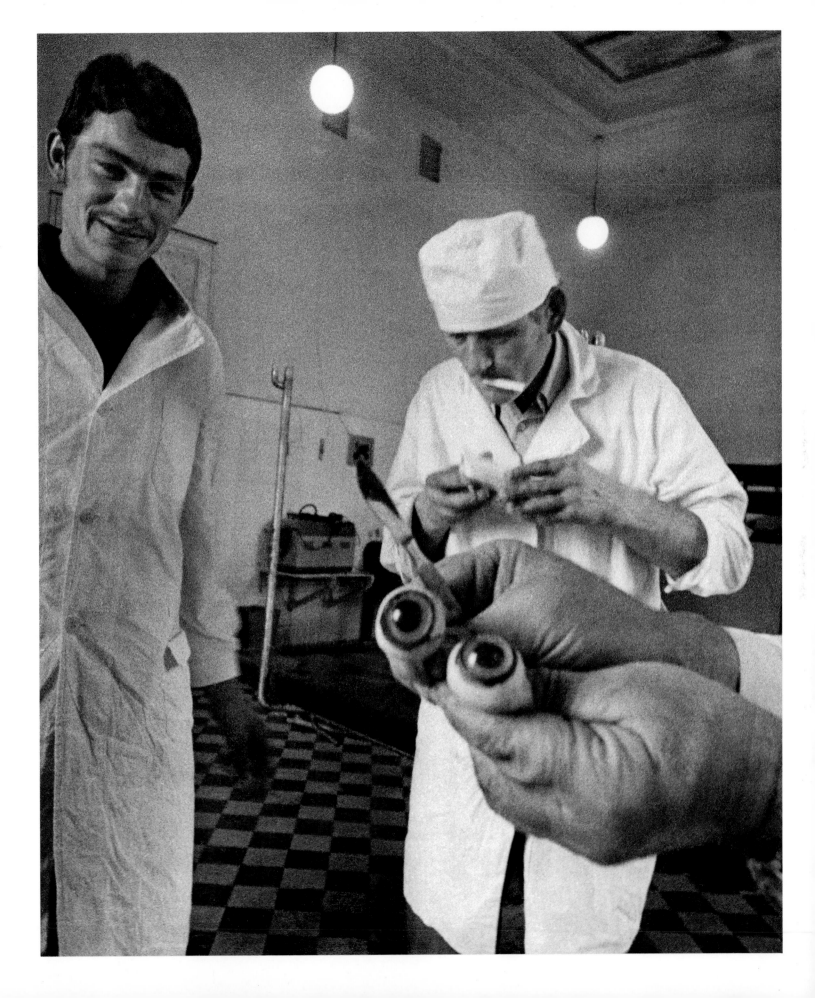

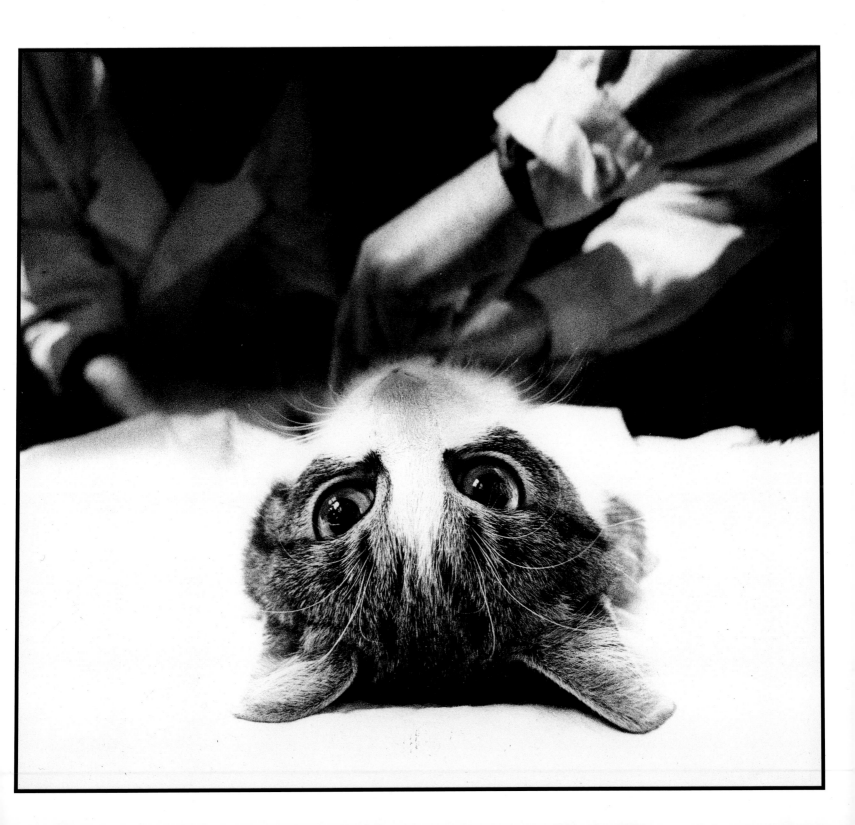

PARADES

Popular rallies and processions have always attracted me. Before a march or a demonstration, the inhabitants of Kaunas would spend a lot of time forming up their ranks, milling around before the festive parade or attempting to keep themselves warm before the October celebrations. Parades have always been occasions for social gatherings, not commemorations of political anniversaries.

The hours leading up to the march itself were always my busiest. I had to get myself in the right place at the right time, where the people, flags, banners and posters were coming together to form a whole, leaving no space unfilled in the viewfinder, so that every smallest part of the eventual picture would inform, narrate or pose a riddle.

People don't just dance, chant slogans or celebrate events in my photographs. Some may watch the merry crowd with a sad smile, for this will be the last such holiday for him or her. They are here to bid farewell to demonstrations and to life. This, at least, is my way of understanding and photographing the scene. Is a holiday truly meaningful if there is not just a little hint of sadness in it? My philosophy is: tell the truth, the whole truth and nothing but the truth, if you are to consider yourself a humanist.

I don't like photographing death. I hate goodbyes. But I treat the theme out of respect and duty to close colleagues and friends. I am happy to say that such farewells have not been too frequent up to now. Long live all my friends and my enemies! Life alone is a thing of some value!

AFTERWORD

Macijauskas and contemporary Soviet photography

Aleksandras Macijauskas's career over the last twenty years has established him as an outstanding figure in contemporary Soviet photography. During that time, his way of looking at the world has been regarded by some as alluring and by others as exasperating; his photographs have provoked both pleasure and repulsion and he himself has been both celebrated and attacked. Yet the influence of his exceptional position has always been acknowledged, despite the fact that he has never sought to impose his techniques of expression on others, cares nothing about being a public figure and has worked without thought for influencing contemporary or future photographers. Although he wishes only to be allowed to develop quietly in his own vein, he has attracted and influenced photographers all over the USSR and with increasing regularity has been recognized by the outside world as perhaps the most striking figure in Soviet photography today.

Macijauskas began to take photographs in the early 1960s, at a time when the Soviet Baltic Republics – Lithuania, Latvia and Estonia – were emerging from the years of rigid repression initiated by Stalin. As they began to take a new interest in the richness of their native traditions, a sense of national identity and cultural self-determination started to flourish. This was reflected in the arts, especially photography, which soon came to assume a central role in this nationwide quest for identity. In the past every Lithuanian, Latvian and Estonian belonged to a choir, and song festivals were not simply impressive manifestations of folk art but also living testimonies to the vigour of native traditions. Now photography took on a similar importance as (so it seemed) every man, woman and child began to carry a camera.

Almost from the beginning, Macijauskas was a leader of this new movement. Gradually the fossilized formulae of the propagandist official photography crumbled as the stiffly efficient heroes of the past and the idealization of the work ethic were confronted with depictions of the intimate sorrows and pleasures of everyday life. Strident celebrations of the new technocratic age were tempered by the reappearance of traditional folk customs and by fresh interest in such themes as country life, celebrations of the beauty and strength of human communities, and the need for harmony between man and nature. This spontaneous photographic movement imbued the optimism of official propaganda with a truly national spirit and challenged the harshness, emotional sterility and depersonalization of photography of the time. No wonder, therefore, that the new photographic activity in the Baltic States often met with mistrust and suspicion; only after many years was it represented in State exhibitions or the press.

The individuality of Macijauskas's work was apparent from the start, even within the context of this major photographic movement in Lithuania. Most of his contemporaries working in the new vein presented their ideals in a highly romantic fashion, celebrating the Baltic regions as the Promised Land and portraying its inhabitants apparently enjoying a life of prelapsarian bliss, untouched by the depravity of the modern world. Macijauskas, in contrast, evoked a world of Gogolian laughter – hearty, often ironic, but never unsympathetic. Like the audience of *The Government Inspector*, viewers of these photographs are told: 'Who are you laughing at? You are laughing at yourselves.'

Macijauskas's first and still unfinished cycle, 'Village Markets', was from its inception an ideal instrument for his metaphorical expression of the truth of contemporary life. It depicts people in a new society struggling for identity in the face of inner inconsistency and a feeling of being out of step with the rest of the world. For Macijauskas, the market-place is an open-air theatre where the drama of life today is staged in miniature. This drama is both comic and tragic and its performers are seen without embellishment: they are good-hearted but grasping, emotional, even tender, but at the same time self-interested, cunning and ruthless. Most of all, they are full to overflowing with energy and the spirit of enterprise.

This folk theatre is reviewed by Macijauskas as if through a magnifying glass: the head of a pig is enlarged to supernatural dimensions; men and women and their purchases – cattle, farm produce, domestic utensils – are turned into wax models by an unusual angle; the steeply convergent perspective of the wide-angle lens gives their postures a startling dynamism. This deliberate distortion, which is used for the sake of metaphysical exaggeration, not only gives the pictures a stylistic unity, but also enables us to see and to correlate several different actions simultaneously. Thus we can observe in the midst of the market-place's chaos – crowds, cars, poultry, cattle, horse-carts, piles of potatoes and heaps of eggs – strange touches of unreality.

Macijauskas's photography has often been compared with the work of the contemporary Russian writer Vasily Shukshin, who is best known outside the

USSR for his stories of village life, although his interest in the relationship between the individual and society ranges more widely. His position in the literary world is certainly comparable with Macijauskas's in photography, but Shukshin's portrayal of rural life is more wistful and nostalgic: Macijauskas in comparison seems less compromising and more aggressive. However, both can be regarded as continuing the Gogolian tradition: admiration and reverence for the common man; tolerance and exuberance in combination; mockery of the autocratic mentality which never ceases to mould the evil-minded and the stupid to suit its narrow vision. Perhaps it is because of this relationship to the Gogolian tradition that both men have been admired and criticized so passionately, although their stature has rarely been questioned.

Macijauskas's account of his upbringing and early life throws into relief important themes in his work. It is surely not by accident that the subjects he treats tend to dwell on two strikingly recurrent topics. The first is cruelty, which is observed with a childlike detachment, although it is allowed to suggest weighty questions about the meaning of life. The second is death, always seen as an omnipresent part of the natural order, but no less a cause of fear for all that. In the 'Village Markets' cycle, the butchered lambs are as meek and peaceful as sleeping babies, yet a cow being led to slaughter raises its head as if to scream aloud. At first glance, the work of the vets in the 'Veterinary Clinic' cycle seems almost brutal, yet their actions are motivated by deep concern for the animals in their care. Such paradoxes are ever-present in Macijauskas's pictures.

As a photographer, he is strangely attracted by crowd scenes – public meetings, people massed like ants. They too, like the village markets, are simply focuses for his metaphorical concerns. The pictures gathered under the title 'Parades' are good examples of this. The people marching are not doing so as a display of united political purpose: they are participating in the folk rituals of a new age. It is the sort of social event with which people in all periods and places have marked the passage of time. The participants look forward to the parades as though they were huge parties, for they are occasions to meet their friends and acquaintances and to note those who are no longer with them. Macijauskas is not simply photographing intriguing details of these events, but also observing the inception of a new tradition. The pictures of funerals take this process a step further in their depiction of the rituals of death.

The cycle 'Summer' is perhaps more critical: people stream to the seaside to escape their daily routines and to come closer to nature, but in fact they are also undergoing yet another struggle for space in which to live. As they rid themselves of one set of relationships that has been imposed on them, without thinking they acquire a different one. Like all Macijauskas's cycles, it is really part of a larger whole, of which the 'Village Markets' and 'Veterinary Clinic' projects are the centrepiece. The tone may vary: there is an element of drama in the 'Veterinary Clinic' series that is outweighed by humorous exaggeration in the 'Village Markets', but all share an interest in men's and women's emotional attachment to the world of nature, of which they are irretrievably a part.

Today Aleksandras Macijauskas is both a celebrity in the USSR and the best-known contemporary Soviet photographer in the world. He would never have reached this position if the spontaneous flourishing of Lithuanian photographers in the 1960s had not led to the establishment in 1969 of the Photography Art Society of the Lithuanian SSR, of which Macijauskas was one of the founders. Long before Gorbachev's new model of socialist enterprise and the proclamation of *perestroika* and *glasnost*, the Society provided Macijauskas and other Lithuanian photographers with an economically self-sufficient and independent basis. This was essential for the development of any widespread photographic culture. There is nothing like the Society anywhere else in the USSR. It provides regular publicity for its members, both in the press and by means of exhibitions, and offers financial backing for projects, an education programme and international contacts. The Society maintains several photo-galleries and libraries as well as a school and a large collection of photographs. Regular seminars, symposia and festivals are held and attract much attention from other states in the USSR. With Antanas Sutkus, Macijauskas has been co-organizer of all these activities since the Society's inception.

The lead provided by the Baltic photographers was a crucial inspiration for the new Soviet photography of the 1970s. This success is in large part due to Macijauskas. Once he remarked that 'optimism means a way of life, not just jolly people'. This is a good statement of the underlying philosophy by which he and other Lithuanian photographers have been guided. It has enabled them to challenge successfully the superficial propagandist clichés normally employed for representing the happy and satisfying life of a socialist country. Together they have altered the course of contemporary Soviet photography away from official styles towards a more forthright means of expression.

Daniela Mrázková and Vladimír Remeš

Exhibitions

O = one-man exhibition

G = group exhibition

PI = participation on personal invitation

1968	**O**	Čiurlionis Museum, Kaunas, Lithuania
1969	**G**	*Nine Lithuanian Photographers*, Journalists' Union Exhibition Hall, Moscow, USSR
1969	**O**	Journalists' Union Exhibition Hall, Moscow, USSR
1970	**O**	Malá Galeria, Bratislava, Czechoslovakia
1970	**O**	Art Museum, Ružomberok, Czechoslovakia
1974	**G**	*Four Lithuanian Photographers*, Photographers' Gallery, London, Great Britain
1974	**O**	Bibliothèque Nationale, Paris, France
1975	**O**	*Village Markets*, Hôtel de Ville, Arles, France
1976	**O**	Galeria Fotografiki, Warsaw, Poland
1976	**O**	Galeria Fotografiki, Krakow, Poland
1977	**O**	Musée Réattu, Arles, France
1978	**PI**	*18 Photographes européens*, Centre d'Art Contemporain, Brussels, Belgium
1979	**PI**	*Contemporary European Photography*, Biennale, Venice, Italy

1979	G	*Lithuanian Photography*, Canon Photo Gallery, Amsterdam, The Netherlands
1979	O	Art Research Institute, Moscow, USSR
1979	O	*The Veterinary Clinic*, Prakapas Gallery, New York, USA
1980	O	Photo Gallery, Kaunas, Lithuania
1980	PI	*Brandt, Giacomelli, Macijauskas*, Centre d'Art Contemporain, Brussels, Belgium
1980	G	*Lithuanian Photography*, Photographers' Gallery, London, Great Britain
1980	O	House of Culture, Burgas, Bulgaria
1980	O	UNO Library, New York, USA
1981	PI	*Three Europeans: Macijauskas, Krzyzanowski, Schurman*, Museum of Modern Art, San Francisco, USA
1981	O	Babylon Cinema, Berlin, West Germany
1982-83	O	Photo galleries throughout Czechoslovakia
1983	PI	*12 Photographes étrangers*, Maison de la Culture, Namur, Belgium
1984	O	Valokuva Galleria Finfoto, Helsinki, Finland
1984	O	Photo Gallery, Kaunas, Lithuania
1984	PI	*Contemporary European Photography*, Benteler Galleries, Houston, USA
1985	G	Museum of Modern Art, San Francisco, USA

1986	G	Centre National de la Photographie, Paris, France
1986	O	Galerie Municipale du Château d'Eau, Toulouse, France
1987	G	*Facets of Modernism*, Museum of Modern Art, San Francisco, USA
1988	O	Photography Museum, Lvov, USSR
1987-88	G	*Another Russia*, Museum of Modern Art, Oxford, Great Britain
1989-90	G	*Photostroika*, Aperture Gallery, New York, USA

Photographs in Public Collections

Bibliothèque Nationale, Paris, France

Canon Photo Gallery, Amsterdam, The Netherlands

Galerie Municipale du Château d'Eau, Toulouse, France

International Center of Photography, New York, USA

Musée d'Art et d'Histoire, Fribourg, Switzerland

Musée Français de la Photographie, Paris, France

Musée Réattu, Arles, France

Museum of Modern Art, San Francisco, USA

Prakapas Gallery, New York, USA

Šiauliai Photography Museum, Lithuania

University Art Museum of New Mexico, USA

Bibliography

Camera International magazine, Paris, 1985 (3)

Coke, Van Deren and du Pont, Diana, *A Facet of Modernism*, Hudson Hills Press, New York, 1986

Demin, V., 'Aleksandras Macijauskas' in *Valokuva* magazine, Helsinki, 1984 (5)

European Photography magazine, Göttingen, 1982 (10); 1986 (2)

Fotografen aus der UdSSR, PIAG, Baden-Baden, 1982

Fotografi magazine, Oslo, 1982 (3)

Fotografia magazine, Warsaw, 1987 (2)

Fotografie magazine, Leipzig, 1982 (7, 10)

Hlaváč Ludovít, *Dějiny fotografie*, Osveta, Martin, 1987

Lemagny, Jean-Claude and Rouille, A., *Histoire de la Photographie*, Bordas, Paris, 1987

Lietuvos fotografija year book, Vaga, Vilnius, 1967, 1968, 1971, 1978

Lietuvos fotografija year book, Mintis, Vilnius, 1982, 1984

Morozov, Sergei, *Tvorcheskaya fotografia*, Planeta, Moscow, 1985

Mrázková, Daniela, *Příběh fotografie*, Mladá fronta, Prague, 1985

Mrázková, Daniela, *Masters of Photography: A Thematic History*, Hamlyn, London, 1987

Mrázková, Daniela, 'Macijauskas: freska života' in *Československá fotografie* magazine, Prague, 1988 (5)

Mrázková, Daniela, 'Many Nations, Many Voices' in *Aperture* magazine, no. 116, New York, 1989

Mrázková, Daniela and Remeš, Vladimír, *Another Russia*, Thames and Hudson, London, 1986

Photo Communiqué magazine, Toronto, 1982 (3)

Photography Year Book, Fountain Press, London, 1972, 1974, 1978

Rosenblum, Naomi, *A World History of Photography*, Abbeville Press, New York, 1984

Saschin, A., 'Interview with A. Macijauskas' in *Journalist* magazine, Moscow, 1975 (5)

Stigneev, V., 'Novoe reshenie' in *Sovetskoe foto* magazine, Moscow, 1978 (2)

Thornton, G., 'Veterinarian in Close-Up' in *The New York Times*, November 11, 1979

Vartanov, Anri, *Fotografija: dokument i obraz*, Planeta, Moscow, 1985